D0990731

SWINGING FOR THE FENCES

LIFE IN THE NEGRO LEAGUES

BARNSTORMING

MICHAEL DeMOCKER

PURPLE TOAD PUBLISHING

HALF HOLLOW HILLS
COMMUNITY LIBRARY
55 VANDERBILT PKWY
DIX HILLS, NY 11746

Copyright © 2017 by Purple Toad Publishing, Inc. All rights reserved. No part of this book may be reproduced without written permission from the publisher. Printed and bound in the United States of America.

Printing   1   2   3   4   5   6   7   8   9

PUBLISHER'S NOTE
This series, Swinging for the Fences: Life in the Negro Leagues, covers racism in United States history and how it affected professional baseball. Some of the events told in this series may be disturbing to young readers.

SWINGING FOR THE
FENCES
LIFE IN THE
NEGRO LEAGUES

A 4 VOL. SERIES

A Whole New League
by Wayne L. Wilson
Barnstorming
by Michael DeMocker
Legends of the Leagues
by Pete DiPrimio
Breaking the Barriers
by Russell Roberts

ABOUT THE AUTHOR
Michael DeMocker is a New Orleans-based writer, photojournalist and former first baseman who was born in the backseat of his parents' car outside the minor league baseball stadium in Rochester, New York (really).

Publisher's Cataloging-in-Publication Data
DeMocker, Michael.
  Barnstorming / written by Michael DeMocker.
    p. cm.
Includes bibliographic references, glossary, and index.
ISBN 9781624692802
1. Negro leagues—History—Juvenile literature. 2. Baseball—United States—History—Juvenile literature. I. Series: Swinging For The Fences : Life in the Negro Leagues.
 GV865.A1 2017
 796.357
Library of Congress Control Number: 2016937176
ebook ISBN: 9781624692819

TICKETS

Chapter One
Barnstorming Begins   4

Chapter Two
Blocked at the Plate   12

Chapter Three
A Hard Road   18
Side Trip   23

Chapter Four
Game Day   24

Chapter Five
Famous Barnstorming Teams   32

Timeline   40

Chapter Notes   42

Works Consulted   44

Further Reading   44

On the Internet   45

Glossary   46

Index   48

BEGINS

CHAPTER ONE

The rumbling bus hit a pothole, jarring the young man awake. It was getting light outside. As they passed a cornfield, he could just make out a scarecrow wearing a weathered red ball cap. The young man wondered where they could be as he and his baseball team rode through the dawn to reach their next game. He was sore from last night's game, and dozing on the hard wooden bench of the bus didn't help.

As he tried to go back to sleep, he thought of the game they had just played. Ten thousand faces, black and white, had cheered as his team of African-American players beat a local semi-pro team of white players. He had stolen bases and between innings had juggled baseballs to entertain the kids gathered at the fence. When the dust had settled, his team had won again. Of course, they usually won.

Barnstorming teams like the Indianapolis Clowns spent a great deal of time on buses, traveling from town to town to play their games.

Many restaurants were owned by people who turned away African Americans, refusing them service.

Then, as the sun sank over the baseball diamond, he had loaded his bat, glove, and baseball shoes onto the bus. Since there were no restaurants in town that would serve a black man, he had to eat his dinner of sardines and beans out of a mason jar he carried with him. While the bus bounced and rocked, he and his fellow players had teased the bus driver, played cards, and sung songs until they finally fell asleep.

Soon they would play again, and then get back on the old bus to continue to the next small town and the next game. For an African-American baseball player in the early 1900s, this was a way to make money playing the game he loved: baseball.

This was barnstorming.

In the early nineteenth century, the term *barnstorming* referred to traveling theater troupes. They would rent out a farmer's barn and sell

tickets for a show. Later, a barnstorming event could be a stunt airplane show or a politician traveling from one town to another, looking for votes. It was also used to describe African-American baseball events. These shows gave fans a chance to watch African-Americans play baseball after they were banned from playing in the white professional leagues.

Barnstorming teams played between 50 and 150 games a season all across the United States and Canada. In the fall and winter, when the weather turned cold, the teams headed south to Florida, Mexico, and Cuba.

The term *barnstorming* came to describe stunt airplane shows, as well as baseball games played by traveling teams.

During the age of barnstorming, there was no schedule like there is today, and teams were very busy trying to arrange games. The barnstorming teams played against all kinds of opponents, from semi-pro to professional teams. Booking agents would arrange the games and take a cut of the ticket sales. Sometimes a booking agent would even drive the bus to

★★★

Young fans flocked to see baseball legends like Josh Gibson when the players barnstormed through their town. Gibson had a remarkable .359 batting average during his Negro League career. In 1972, he became the second Negro League player inducted into the Baseball Hall of Fame.

★★★

the game. Since the teams made money only if they played, they played as often as they could.

The games were very popular. In modern times, local baseball teams play nearly every day, half the time at home and the other half on the road. Barnstorming games were special events that only came through town every so often. Thousands of baseball fans would pay to watch famous Negro League players. In some towns, the barnstorming players would be the first African-Americans the white residents had ever seen.[1]

How did barnstorming begin?

In 1887, John "Bud" Fowler, one of the first black players to play professionally, left the International League team in Binghamton, New York. White teammates and white opponents had become increasingly upset at sharing the field with black players. They threatened not to play if black players were on the field. Fowler would not stand for the racism.

Two weeks after he and a teammate left the team, the league's white owners voted to "approve of no more contracts with colored

John "Bud" Fowler (back row, center), seen here with the Keokuk, Iowa, team he joined in 1885.

ANSON,
(1st Base, CHICAGO.

CHICAGO

OLD JUDGE & GYPSY QUEEN CIGARETTES

In 1887, star Chicago first baseman Cap Anson refused to take the field for an exhibition game in Newark, New Jersey, because the opposing team had a black pitcher and catcher. This was not the first time Anson had complained about playing against minorities. His star power led several players and owners to jump on the segregation bandwagon. Soon, a "Gentlemen's Agreement" banned contracts for black players.

men."[2] This unofficial Gentlemen's Agreement kept African-Americans from joining professional baseball teams.

In response, Fowler founded the first black traveling team: the New York Gorhams. The team played all over the country to great acclaim. Whenever Fowler found himself without a team, he formed another barnstorming club to make money well into fall.

One of his most popular teams was the All-American Black Tourists, which he organized in 1899. The team would arrive in a special railroad car, dressed in fancy black suits with top hats and umbrellas. Fowler

told the opposing team that if they asked, "We will play the game in these suits."[3]

If Fowler had been white, he likely would have had a long and stable professional career in baseball. As he once wrote, "My skin is against me. If I had not been quite so black, I might have caught on as a Spaniard or something of that kind. The race prejudice is so strong that my black skin barred me."[4]

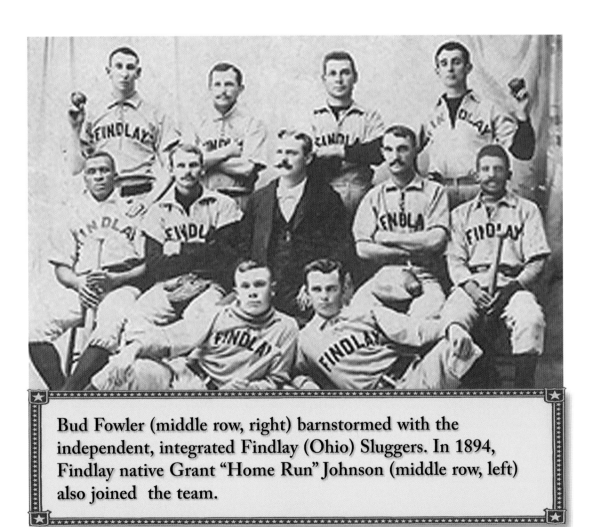

Bud Fowler (middle row, right) barnstormed with the independent, integrated Findlay (Ohio) Sluggers. In 1894, Findlay native Grant "Home Run" Johnson (middle row, left) also joined the team.

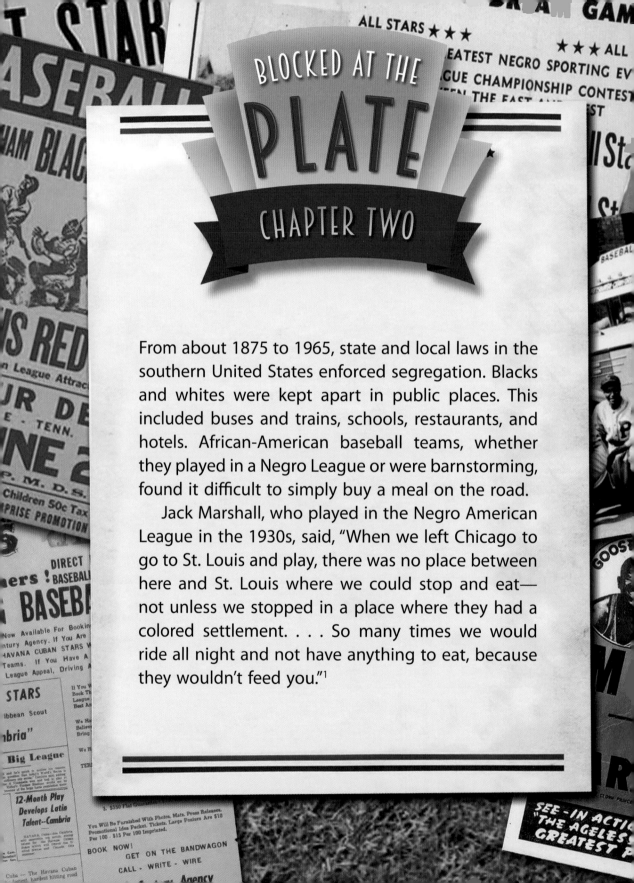

BLOCKED AT THE PLATE

CHAPTER TWO

From about 1875 to 1965, state and local laws in the southern United States enforced segregation. Blacks and whites were kept apart in public places. This included buses and trains, schools, restaurants, and hotels. African-American baseball teams, whether they played in a Negro League or were barnstorming, found it difficult to simply buy a meal on the road.

Jack Marshall, who played in the Negro American League in the 1930s, said, "When we left Chicago to go to St. Louis and play, there was no place between here and St. Louis where we could stop and eat— not unless we stopped in a place where they had a colored settlement. . . . So many times we would ride all night and not have anything to eat, because they wouldn't feed you."[1]

A segregated waiting room at a Durham, North Carolina bus station. Barnstorming players faced many difficulties and indignities when traveling for games.

Buck Leonard's batting average through 14 seasons with the Homestead Grays was .320. He often batted fourth, behind Josh Gibson.

He went on to tell how players would fill up jars with beans or sardines to snack on during a long trip. Sometimes, a scheduling mix-up would leave the team with no game—which meant no money to buy food or travel to the next town.

Walter Fenner "Buck" Leonard, who has been called the black Lou Gehrig, barnstormed with the famed Homestead Grays in the 1930s. He remembers the challenges African-American teams faced on the road. "We played a different game in a different town every night. That meant a lot of riding, a lot of playing, and a lot of staying in second-rate hotels and eating on the run. We couldn't stay in good hotels, and the meals were bad. Down South, and in some northern cities, we couldn't eat in white restaurants or stay in white hotels. In places where there were not any black hotels or restaurants, we stayed in rooming houses or in the YMCA. And sometimes we slept on the bus. But we didn't care about that. We loved the game and we wanted to play."[2]

Leonard, who was elected to the Baseball Hall of Fame in 1972, remembered how there were often players on teams who were light-

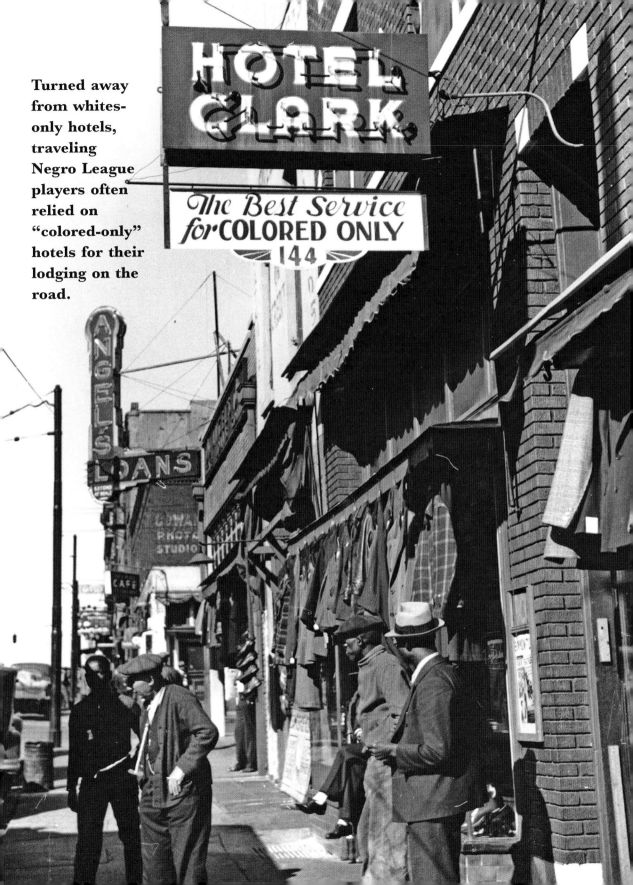

Turned away from whites-only hotels, traveling Negro League players often relied on "colored-only" hotels for their lodging on the road.

skinned enough to pass as white. That player could get away with buying sandwiches for the whole team from a whites-only restaurant. Sometimes hotels where his team had planned to stay turned them away when they arrived. The hotel did not know they would be renting rooms to black men.

In addition to sleeping at hotels and rooming houses where blacks where allowed to stay, players would also stay at the homes of black families who would host them when they played in town. The Kansas City Monarchs' answer to the problem was to simply camp out. They would pull tents and bedding from their cars and set up a camp kitchen. They would even hunt wild game for their meals.

When traveling and playing south of the border in Mexico or in Central and South America, players generally avoided the racism they

Jim Crow laws required the separation of the races in public places. Cabins like these in 1939 South Carolina were some of the few places black players could spend the night on the road.

In 1937, dictator General Rafael Trujillo brought Josh Gibson (back row, left), Satchel Paige (center row, right) and Cool Papa Bell (front row, center) down to the Dominican Republic to win the championship for his Ciudad Trujillo Dragons. Then he reportedly jailed the team the night before the crucial seventh game so that the players couldn't stay out too late. The Dragons won the championship, and the Negro League players returned to America.

faced in the United States. They could experience the comforts that they couldn't at home, like eating in nice restaurants and staying in fancy hotels. But upon returning to the United States, they once again faced segregation and hardships.

Judy Johnson, who played on the greatest Negro League teams of the 1920s and 1930s, remembered the change that came over him upon getting off the bus after a difficult journey. "We would get tired from the riding, we would fuss like a bunch of chickens, but when you put that suit [baseball uniform] on it was different. We just knew that was your job and you'd just do it. We used to have a lot of fun, and there were some sad days too, but there was always sun shining someplace."[3]

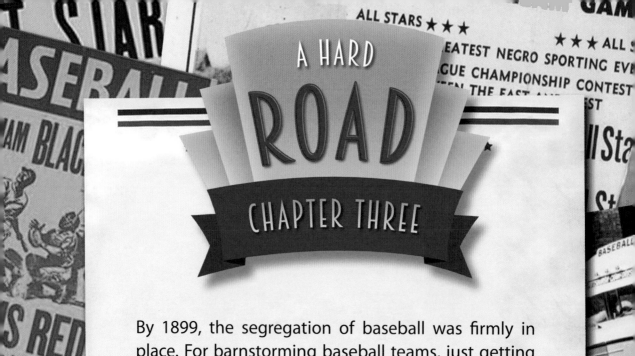

A HARD ROAD

CHAPTER THREE

By 1899, the segregation of baseball was firmly in place. For barnstorming baseball teams, just getting from town to town could be a challenge, especially before there were buses. Arthur W. Hardy barnstormed from 1906 until 1912. He talked about traveling with the Kansas City Giants: "We got around any way we could. I have ridden between towns, especially out in Kansas and Nebraska where they were off the railroads—there weren't any buses then—in a farm wagon. Any kind of transportation. I've ridden in a wagon fifteen or twenty miles and then slept all night in a railroad station to catch a train to get to the next place."[1] When they slept in train stations, players used their clothes as a bed.

Players would pack themselves into cars and drive hundreds of miles, play a game, and return

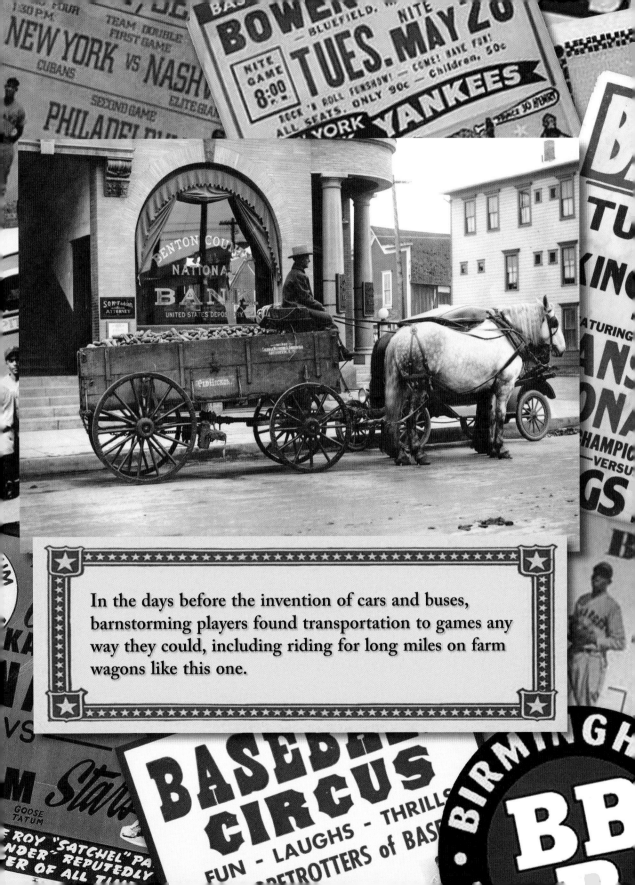

In the days before the invention of cars and buses, barnstorming players found transportation to games any way they could, including riding for long miles on farm wagons like this one.

Judy Johnson was one of the best third basemen in the league. His lifetime batting average was .290. He later became the first African-American spring training coach in baseball in 1954. In 1975, he was elected to the Baseball Hall of Fame.

home again all in one day. Judy Johnson, who played for the Homestead Grays out of Pittsburgh, described those times: "Every day you were going, you'd go and ride over those hills. Every two hours you had to average a hundred miles. With nine men in the car!"[2] Cars, of course, would break down, and some of the players had to catch up later, after their car was fixed. The teams would start their games short-handed.

In the later years of barnstorming, the teams sometimes had their own bus. If the noisy, uncomfortable box broke down, the long trips would be miserable. It was hard to get comfortable on the wooden seats of the bus. Players passed the time by playing cards, throwing dice, or even singing.

Buck Leonard wrote about singing on the long bus trips: "What we specialized in was barbershop singing, four-part harmony, and we sang just about every night when we were traveling. It sounded good late at night, and it seemed like it made the trips a little shorter. Sometimes we would all be singing, and we would keep singing until we fell off to sleep."[3] Teasing the bus driver was another way to pass they time, he added.[4]

Singing was a way players passed the time on long road trips. Negro League pitcher Charley Pride would sing and play guitar on the bus and before games. After his baseball career, he became a famous country singer. In 2000, he was inducted into the Country Music Hall of Fame.

The rough travel was so hard, some players quit because of it. As one former player said, "The nights weren't long enough. You were just as tired the next day as when you went to bed the night before."[5]

The players used all kinds of vehicles to travel between games, from farm wagons to overloaded cars to trucks that looked like covered wagons. But some players traveled much more comfortably. The Homestead Grays rode to games in a Ford bus they named *Blue Goose*. Not to be outdone by their cross-town rivals, the Pittsburgh Crawfords traveled in a General Motors bus. It was considered the coolest team bus of the 1930s.[6]

The famous pitcher Robert Leroy "Satchel" Paige had a private plane to fly him from game to game. The Page Fence Giants traveled in a special 60-foot train car with a dining room and cook, a sleeping area, and even a barber. This made it easier for the players in an era when African Americans could not get served in most restaurants or hotels.

Barnstorming players on the 1946 Satchel Paige All-Stars traveled in style aboard a special airplane. Paige himself is peering out on the right side of the plane's doorway.

Side Trip

Buck O'Neil, a Negro League player and manager, tells the story about his teammate Satchel Paige on a barnstorming trip to Charleston, South Carolina. Paige invited him on a side trip to fill free time because their hotel rooms weren't ready. They took a boat to a part of Charleston that had been a major port and market for slaves arriving by ship from Africa.

A plaque on a tree marked where slaves where sold into a lifetime of toil and bondage. The two players stood in silence for a while before Paige commented, "I feel like I been here before. My grandmother or my grandfather could have been auctioned off here."

"That was Robert Leroy Paige," "O'Neil later said. "A little bit deeper than most people thought."

An artist's illustration of a slave auction.

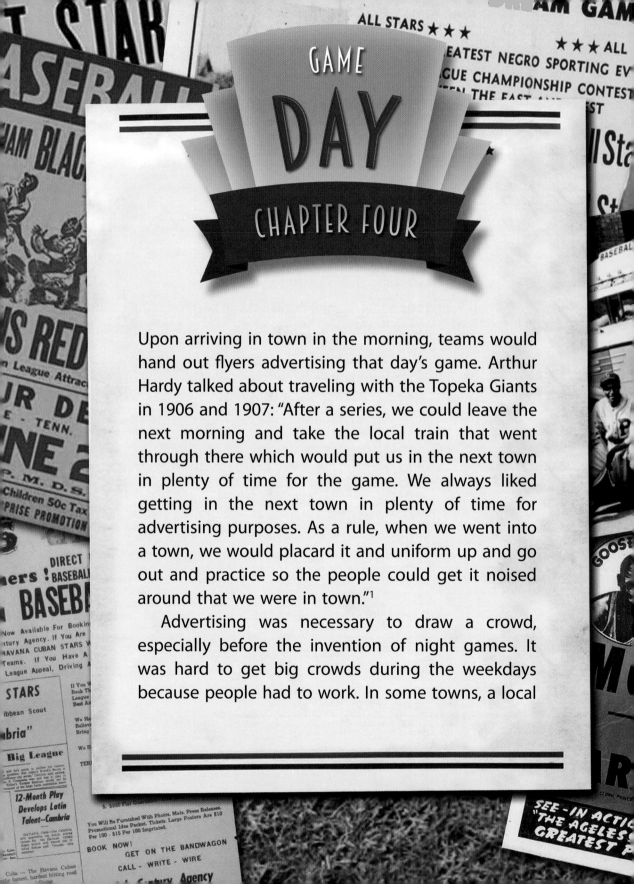

GAME

DAY

CHAPTER FOUR

Upon arriving in town in the morning, teams would hand out flyers advertising that day's game. Arthur Hardy talked about traveling with the Topeka Giants in 1906 and 1907: "After a series, we could leave the next morning and take the local train that went through there which would put us in the next town in plenty of time for the game. We always liked getting in the next town in plenty of time for advertising purposes. As a rule, when we went into a town, we would placard it and uniform up and go out and practice so the people could get it noised around that we were in town."[1]

Advertising was necessary to draw a crowd, especially before the invention of night games. It was hard to get big crowds during the weekdays because people had to work. In some towns, a local

OPENING THE 1942 BASEBALL SEASON!

Kansas City Monarchs
– VERSUS –
Memphis Red Sox

DOUBLEHEADER

RUPPERT STADIUM
22nd and Brooklyn
SUNDAY, MAY 17
First Game . . . 2:00 P. M.
Pre-Game Activities . . . 1:45 P. M.
CEREMONY BETWEEN GAMES

General Admission . . 55¢ tax inc.
Box Seats . . 25¢ extra

Advertisements like this one for a Negro League doubleheader played in Brooklyn, New York were an important way that barnstorming teams filled the stands for their games.

band would lead both teams on a parade through the streets to the baseball field. Admission to the games was 25 cents for kids (the cost of a meal for a player) and 50 cents to 75 cents for adults (about the cost of a player's hotel room for the night).[2]

Barnstorming games were not always played on the best of fields. Sometimes, a rough sandlot or a grassy meadow with bases thrown down was the only place to play. The players often had to set up a field before a game could start.

A barnstorming team had fewer players than a regular major league team. If a player got hurt on these rough fields, they often just had to play through the pain. Since pitchers could not pitch every day, a pitcher who was on a rest day would sometimes be in charge of selling tickets at the gate. Barnstorming players got paid only if the game was played. They did not cancel games even for heavy rain or other bad weather.

Hinchliffe Stadium remains in Paterson, New Jersey — the former home of the New York Black Yankees and the New York Cubans.

The schedule for a barnstorming team could be grueling. "We would play one team today, then play another team tomorrow," said Buck Leonard of the Homestead Grays. "We would even go up into Lewiston, Maine; Manchester, New Hampshire; and Lynn, Massachusetts. Some of them had county fairs in the summertime, and we'd play on Saturday night. We would stay up there about two weeks, just playing different white teams around in county fairs and get about a hundred dollars a day. And that was all right."[3]

Players knew that their barnstorming games had to be entertaining. Some were more like a visiting carnival than a contest between a popular "home team" and an out-of-town rival. To make the game more exciting, players stole bases more often,

John Jordan "Buck" O'Neil was a talented player and manager who became a popular speaker about the experiences of Negro League players. He was awarded the Presidential Medal of Freedom a few months after his death in 2006.

and they clowned around. The antics were also a way to lighten the mood. There was always the chance of a racial fight starting when a local white team faced a superior team of African-American players.[4]

Willis Jones (far left, middle row) also played for the St. Paul Colored Gophers in 1907.

Crowds would laugh when players ran the wrong way around the bases after a home run, or a batter swung the bat with only one hand. If an umpire called a very low pitch a strike, a batter might get on his knees for the next pitch.

A player named Willis Jones of the Union Giants would sometimes go into the outfield with a newspaper and pretend to read it during the game. Players also played shadow ball, where they would warm up before a game by pretending to throw around an invisible ball. They would move so quickly and with such realism, fans thought they were using a real ball that was just too fast to see.

In exhibition games, famed pitcher Satchel Paige would sometimes clear the field. He would bring his outfielders in to sit by the mound or tell his infielders to go into the dugout, leaving him to strike out batters with no defense behind him. This, of course, was very entertaining to watch and was one of the reasons many people, black and white, came out to see him play.

The Indianapolis Clowns featured players Spec Bebop and Richard "King Tut" King, who would perform skits that drew huge crowds to the games. Another player on the Clowns,

Richard "King Tut" King

Reece "Goose" Tatum was a Negro League first baseman. His antics during baseball games — like wearing a dress, catching balls behind his back, and inviting fans onto the field during games — landed him a job with the famed Harlem Globetrotters touring basketball team.

Goose Tatum, liked to use a comically huge first baseman's glove. He would also banter with the crowd or opposing players, and was even known to wear a dress instead of a uniform. Sometimes late in a game, Spec Bebop, King Tut, and Goose Tatum would pretend they were fishing in the infield as the game went on around them.

A famously entertaining barnstorming troupe of about three dozen people traveled around Canada in 1929. Two teams called the New York All-Stars and the Texas Giants (who were actually from Chicago) traveled in four trucks that looked like the covered wagons the settlers of the West used a century before. They would set up in a town and offer a 500 dollar prize if the local baseball team could beat them. Of course, since the barnstorming team provided the umpire, it was guaranteed they would never lose their 500 dollars! Later in the day, the troupe would charge people to see the All-Stars and Giants play.

One of the players and organizers, Jack Marshall, talked about the carnival atmosphere that would take over after those games: "Now, when this ballgame was over, then the midway would open up

In 1942, Satchel Paige (left) faced Josh Gibson in the Negro Leagues World Series. Paige heard that Gibson said he could hit Paige. Late in a close game, Paige came in, loaded the bases to reach Gibson, and told the slugger, "I'm gonna throw you fastballs at the knees. Let's see if you can hit one." He struck Gibson out.

again. Now when the midway closes, then the band would play for the dance. That's another admission, and the dance would go on till one o'clock. . . . People got a big kick out of it. And we spread a lot of goodwill up there."[5]

Not every barnstorming game was as much of a carnival as the troupe of New York All-Stars and Texas Giants, but entertainment was definitely part of the business. As the other organized Negro Leagues were formed, such comic displays were considered unprofessional and were no longer performed.

Barnstorming teams usually made sure not to win by too many runs. They tried to keep the game exciting because they wanted people (and their money) to come back to the ballpark when the team came through town again. However, if the opposing team made racist comments, it was not unheard of for the visitors to run up the score.

Connie Johnson, who played for the Kansas City Monarchs, said that if racist comments were heard, the team would "run twenty, twenty-five runs on 'em, so they'd leave the park whispering."[6]

Despite the segregation of the time, blacks and whites would sometimes share a cookout in a post-game celebration. On the field, however, the black teams and the white teams did not socialize much. Buck Leonard remembers, "At that time, there was not any fraternizing between blacks and whites. We came out and played a ball game and they went their way and we went ours. We didn't talk before the game and didn't do much talking during the ball game. We blacks had an inferiority complex. We felt the only reason they were playing against us was to make money. And we knew the only reason that we were playing them was to make money. That's the way it was."[7]

FAMOUS BARNSTORMING TEAMS

CHAPTER FIVE

Barnstorming teams brought Negro League baseball to fans across the country and into Canada, Mexico, and the Caribbean. They had names like the Cuban X Giants, the Indianapolis Clowns, and the Colored House of David.

The All Nations barnstorming team toured the country with a roster of black, white, Asian, and Native American players. Sponsored by a sporting goods company from Iowa, they played off and on between 1912 and 1925. Often they would have a band play and people could dance. Wrestling shows were staged along with the games.

The 25th Infantry Wreckers was a team drawn from black U.S. Army soldiers. Based in Hawaii and then Arizona, the Wreckers beat military, college,

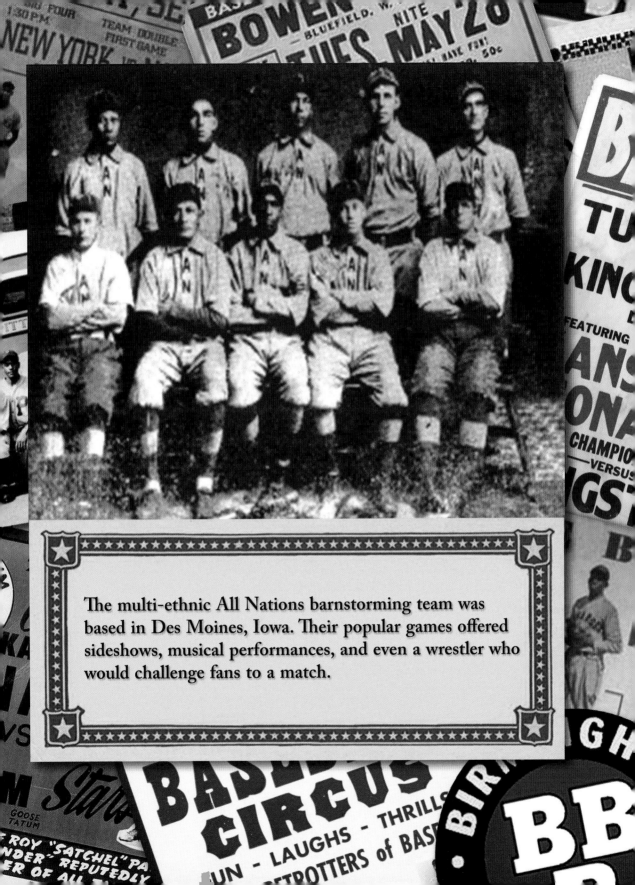

The multi-ethnic All Nations barnstorming team was based in Des Moines, Iowa. Their popular games offered sideshows, musical performances, and even a wrestler who would challenge fans to a match.

The 25th Infantry Wreckers featured future Hall of Famer Charles Wilber "Bullet" Rogan, aka Wilber Joe Rogan— inducted in 1998.

and professional teams all over the country, especially from 1915 until 1921. The soldiers would provide their own uniforms. They would cut the heels off their army-issued boots to make baseball shoes.[1] Pitcher Wilber "Bullet" Rogan, a future Baseball Hall of Famer, played for the Wreckers from 1915 until 1920. After that, he became a Negro League star as a player and manager.

From 1895 until 1898, the Page Fence Giants were a barnstorming team out of Adrian, Michigan. They played in over 100 towns throughout the Midwest. They took on other black teams as well as white teams from the professional league. In 1897, they played 137

games, winning 82 games in a row and losing only 12 times the entire season.

The Homestead Grays were formed from the Blue Ribbons, a group of black steelworkers from Homestead, Pennsylvania, near Pittsburgh. Former player Cumberland Posey organized the team in 1912 and took them barnstorming across the country. Posey managed to attract some of the game's greatest players. The Grays entered the organized American Negro League and then the East-West League. They went back to barnstorming in 1932 after those leagues failed.[2]

The 1913 Homestead Grays. The team's manager and captain, Cumberland Posey, inducted into the Hall of Fame in 2006, is the third man from the left in the second row.

The 1944 Grays won the Negro League World Series. (left to right): Jelly Jackson, Ray Battle, Edward Robinson, Sam Bankhead, Josh Gibson, Buck Leonard, Dave Hoskins, Jerry Benjamin, and Cool Papa Bell

As the team traveled all over the East, they beat nearly every opponent. The Grays finally entered the Negro National League in 1935, where they won nine championships. At some point in their careers, half of the Negro League players now in the Baseball Hall of Fame played for the Homestead Grays.

A man named William Augustus "Gus" Greenlee formed another of the greatest barnstorming teams. A native of North Carolina and a World War I veteran, Greenlee owned a popular restaurant and jazz club in Pittsburgh. Called the Crawford Grill, this club attracted popular African-American entertainers, including

Gus Greenlee

Jazz singer and civil rights activist Lena Horne's trademark song was "Stormy Weather." She threw out the first ball at the 1945 Negro Leagues All-Star Game.

singer and actress Lena Horne and jazz musician Duke Ellington. In addition to the Crawford Grill, Greenlee made his money from gambling and other somewhat shady businesses. In 1931 he used his wealth to buy a local semi-pro baseball team. He reorganized the team into the Pittsburgh Crawfords, or the Craws, hoping to compete with the Homestead Grays.

Duke Ellington composed many classic songs, including "It Don't Mean a Thing if It Ain't Got That Swing"and "Satin Doll." He got to know many Negro League stars as they would come to hear him play after their games.

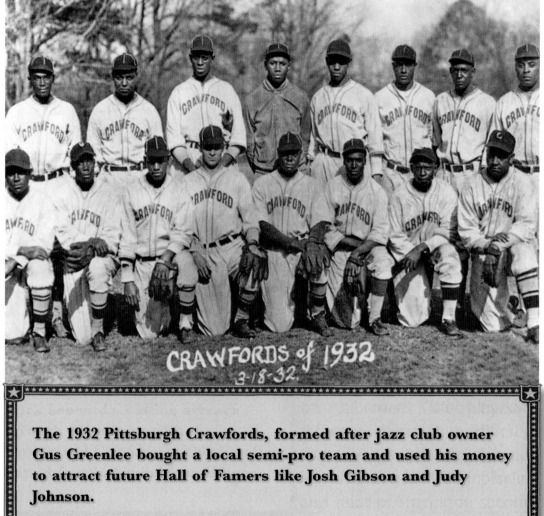

The 1932 Pittsburgh Crawfords, formed after jazz club owner Gus Greenlee bought a local semi-pro team and used his money to attract future Hall of Famers like Josh Gibson and Judy Johnson.

With Greenlee's money, the Craws were able to sign such greats as James Thomas "Cool Papa" Bell, Josh Gibson, and Satchel Paige. They became what some consider the greatest baseball team of all time. They drove across the country in a fancy team bus, playing in exhibition games and games against other Negro League opponents. Despite their fame and success, racism still ruled. They found it hard to find restaurants where they could eat and hotels where they could sleep.

By the early 1940s, teams like the Kansas City Monarchs and the Homestead Grays were very successful. The Negro Leagues were growing more organized, which brought them more success. Money began pouring into the Negro Leagues, and barnstorming was no longer the only way to watch star black athletes play the game.

Jackie Robinson finally broke the major league color barrier on April 15, 1947, by playing his first game with the Brooklyn Dodgers. He was the first African-American to return to the major leagues since the Gentlemen's Agreement was made. Once the door was open, the best players of the Negro Leagues began to sign with major league teams. Barnstorming was over, and baseball players, regardless of race, began to play as one.

Integration was proudly on display at the 1950 All-Star Game. (left to right) Jackie Robinson, Larry Doby, Don Newcombe, Luke Easter, and Roy Campanella relax for a photo.

1887 Professional baseball bans contracts to black players. John "Bud" Fowler forms the first black traveling team, the New York Gorhams.

1895 Fowler's famed Page Fence Giants play their first game.

1896 Racial segregation in public facilities is made legal when the U.S. Supreme Court upholds *Plessy v. Ferguson*.

1912 Cumberland Posey forms Homestead Grays.

1920 The Negro National League is formed, playing until 1931.

Women are allowed to vote as the 19th amendment is ratified.

1923 The Eastern Colored League is formed, playing until 1928.

1924 The first Negro World Series is played between the Kansas City Monarchs and the Hilldale club.

1927 Charles Lindbergh makes the first solo nonstop flight across the Atlantic Ocean.

1928 At 23 years old Walter Diemer creates a recipe for the world's first bubble gum.

1929 The stock market crashes, triggering the Great Depression.

1931 William Augustus "Gus" Greenlee forms Pittsburgh Crawfords.

The Empire State Building is completed.

1932 The Negro Southern League is the sole African-American league in operation.

Amelia Earhart is the first woman to fly solo across the Atlantic.

1933 A new Negro National League is formed, playing until 1948.

1934 Jazz singer Ella Fitzgerald debuts at Harlem's Apollo Theater.

1936 Track-and-field star Jesse Owens stuns Adolf Hitler's Third Reich by winning four gold medals at the Olympic Games in Germany.

1937 The Negro American League is created from western and southern teams.

Josh Gibson and Buck Leonard help the Homestead Grays win the first of their nine Negro National League championships.

1938 Superman debuts in Action Comics

1939 Germany invades Poland, beginning World War II.

1941 The United States enters World War II.

1945 World War II ends and the United Nations is founded.

1947 Jackie Robinson signs with the Brooklyn Dodgers, breaking baseball's color barrier. Larry Doby becomes the first Negro League player in the American League by joining the Detroit Tigers.

1948 At 42 years old, Satchel Paige joins Cleveland Indians.

The Negro National League officially disbands.

1952 The Negro American League folds. More than 150 African-Americans join Major League Baseball.

Chapter 1

1. Donn Rogosin, *Invisible Men: Life in Baseball's Negro Leagues* (New York: Atheneum, 1983), p. 35.

2. Society for American Baseball Research, http://www.sabr.org

3. Robert Peterson, *Only the Ball Was White* (Englewood Cliffs, NJ: Prentice-Hall, 1970), p. 146.

4. Society for American Baseball Research.

Chapter 2

1. Robert Peterson, *Only the Ball Was White* (Englewood Cliffs, NJ: Prentice-Hall, 1970), p. 154.

2. Buck Leonard, with James A. Riley, *Buck Leonard: The Black Lou Gehrig* (New York: Carroll & Graff, 1995), pp. 126–127.

3. Donn Rogosin, *Invisible Men: Life in Baseball's Negro Leagues* (New York: Atheneum, 1983), p. 91.

Chapter 3

1. Robert Peterson, *Only the Ball Was White* (Englewood Cliffs, NJ: Prentice-Hall, 1970), p. 3.

2. Ibid., p. 145.

3. Buck Leonard, with James A. Riley, *Buck Leonard: The Black Lou Gehrig* (New York: Carroll & Graff, 1995), p. 70.

4 Donn Rogosin, *Invisible Men: Life in Baseball's Negro Leagues* (New York: Atheneum, 1983), p. 127.

5 Ibid., p. 78.

6 Ibid., p. 77.

Chapter 4

1. Robert Peterson, *Only the Ball Was White* (Englewood Cliffs, NJ: Prentice-Hall, 1970), p. 147.

2. Ibid., p. 148.

3. Buck Leonard, with James A. Riley, *Buck Leonard: The Black Lou Gehrig* (New York: Carroll & Graff, 1995), p. 62

4. Donn Rogosin, *Invisible Men: Life in Baseball's Negro Leagues* (New York: Atheneum, 1983), p. 141.

5. Peterson, p. 9.

6. Rogosin, p. 121.

7. Leonard, p. 142.

Chapter 5

1. William McNeil, *Black Baseball Out of Season: Pay for Play Outside of the Negro Leagues.* (Jefferson, NC: McFarland, 2012), p. 52.

2. Robert Peterson, *Only the Ball Was White* (Englewood Cliffs, NJ: Prentice-Hall, 1970), p. 92.

Works Consulted

Cieradkowski, Gary. *The League of Outsider Baseball.* New York: Touchstone, 2015.

Foster, Frank. *The Forgotten League: A History of Negro League Baseball.* Anaheim, CA: BookCaps Study Guides, 2012.

Leonard, Buck, with James A. Riley. *Buck Leonard: The Black Lou Gehrig.* New York: Carroll & Graff, 1995.

Major League Baseball: Negro Leagues Legacy
http://mlb.mlb.com/mlb/history/mlb_negro_leagues.jsp

McNeil, William. *Black Baseball Out of Season: Pay for Play Outside of the Negro Leagues.* Jefferson, NC: McFarland, 2012.

Negro League Baseball Players Association. http://www.nlbpa.com

Peterson, Robert. *Only the Ball Was White.* Englewood Cliffs, NJ: Prentice-Hall, 1970.

Rogosin, Donn. *Invisible Men: Life in Baseball's Negro Leagues.* New York: Atheneum, 1983.

Society for American Baseball Research. http://www.sabr.org

Ward, Geoffrey C., Kevin Baker, Ken Burns. *Baseball: An Illustrated History.* New York: Knopf Doubleday Publishing Group, 2010.

Further Reading

Herman, Gail. *Who Was Jackie Robinson?* New York: Grosset & Dunlap, 2010.

Nelson, Kadir. *We Are the Ship: The Story of Negro League Baseball.* New York: Jump At The Sun, 2008.

Rice, Dona Herweck. *Batter Up: History of Baseball.* New York: TIME for Kids, 2012.

Tooke, Wes. *King of the Mound: My Summer with Satchel Paige.* New York: Simon & Schuster Books for Young Readers, 2013. (Fiction.)

On the Internet

Baseball Hall of Fame
   http://baseballhall.org/
Major League Baseball for kids
   http://mlb.mlb.com/mlb/kids/
Negro Leagues Baseball Museum
   http://www.nlbm.com/

Buck Leonard dodges a tag on the bases, 1944.

antics (an-TIKS)—Silly, playful, or funny behavior.

barnstorm (BARN-storm)—To tour an area putting on performances.

booking agent (BUK-ing AY-juhnt)—A person who arranges events for another person or group.

exhibition (ek-suh-BIH-shun)—A game or series that does not count in the official standings or is not part of official league play.

fraternize (FRAT-er-nyz)—To hang out with someone even if it is forbidden.

gentlemen's agreement (JEN-tuhl-munz uh-GREE-muhnt)—A trusted understanding between people that is not legally binding.

inferiority complex (in-feer-ree-AR-ih-tee KOM-pleks)—The feeling of not being as important as someone else.

Jim Crow (JIM KROH)—The type of laws that segregated African-Americans in public places.

midway (MID-WAY)—A path through a fair or carnival where food and amusements are set up.

placard (PLAK-erd)—A sign that is posted or carried for public display.

racism (RAY-sism)—A belief that people who look or act like oneself are better than others, and that it is okay to be mean to those others.

GLOSSARY

segregate (SEH-greh-gayt)—To separate people based on their race, gender, or religion.

semi-pro (SEH-mee PROH)—A league or team in which players are paid, but that is not the players' main job.

shadow ball (SHAD-oh BAWL)—A show put on by players in which they pretend to throw around an invisible ball.

PHOTO CREDITS: P. 5—Electronic Village; pp. 13, 15—Loc.gov; pp. 20, 27, 39, 45—Field of Dreams.it; p. 26—J. Schumaker; p. 38—HSBBT . All other photos—Public Domain. Every measure has been taken to find all copyright holders of material used in this book. In the event any mistakes or omissions have happened within, attempts to correct them will be made in future editions of the book.

25th Infantry Wreckers   32, 34

All-American Black Tourists   10–11

All Nations   32, 33

American Negro League   35

Anson, Cap   10

Bebop, Spec 28, 29

Bell, James Thomas "Cool Papa"   17, 36, 38

Blue Goose   22

Blue Ribbons   35

booking agents   8

Brooklyn Dodgers   39

Colored House of David   32

county fairs   27

Crawford Grill   36–37

Cuban X Giants   32

East-West League   35

Ellington, Duke   37

Fowler, John "Bud"   9–11

Gehrig, Lou   14

Gentlemen's agreement   10, 39

Gibson, Josh   8, 17, 30, 36, 38

Greenlee, William Augustus "Gus"   36–38

Hardy, Arthur W.   18, 24

Harlem Globetrotters   29

Homestead Grays   14, 20, 22, 27, 35, 36, 37, 39

Homestead, Pennsylvania   35

Horne, Lena   37

Indianapolis Clowns   5, 28, 32

International League   9

Jim Crow laws   16

Johnson, Connie   31

Johnson, Grant "Home Run"   11

Johnson, William "Judy"   17, 20

Jones, Willis   28

Kansas City, Giants   18

Kansas City Monarchs   16, 31, 39

King, Richard "King Tut"   28–29

Leonard, Walter Fenner "Buck"   14, 21, 27, 31, 36, 45

Marshall, Jack   12, 30

New York All-Stars   29, 30, 31

New York Gorhams   10

O'Neil, John Jordan "Buck"   23, 27

Page Fence Giants   22, 34

Paige, Satchel   17, 22, 23, 24, 28, 30, 38

Pittsburgh Crawfords   22, 37

Posey, Cumberland   35

Pride, Charlie   21

Robinson, Jackie   39

Rogan, Wilber "Bullet"   34

shadow ball   28

Tatum, Goose   28–29

Texas Giants   29, 31

Topeka Giants   24

Union Giants   28